Visions of Sugarplums

✿ ✿ ✿ ✿ ✿ ✿ ✿ ✿ ✿ ✿

A Collection of Christmas Cookery

Lizzie Norris
Copyright 2007

To order more copies of this e-book contact Lizzie Norris at

adustyframe@yahoo.com

Or visit my website

www.adustyframe.com

Beverages, Appetizers, & Breads

Boston Brown Bread
Yield 4 loaves

2 ½ c. flour

2 ½ c. bran flakes

1 c. raisins

1 tsp. baking soda

1 egg

¾ c. sugar

1 c. dark corn syrup

2 c. buttermilk

1. Preheat oven to 375 F.
2. Mix flour, bran flakes, raisins, and baking soda.
3. Combine egg, sugar, syrup, and buttermilk. Mix until well blended. Stir into the flour mixture. Mix well.
4. Pour batter into 4 well greased and floured 20 oz cans.
   Bake at 375 F for 1 hour. Cool bread in the cans.
   To remove loaf from the can, remove the bottom of the can with a can opener. Push the bread through the can.
5. Wrap to store or freeze.

To make "buttermilk" add 1 Tb of lemon juice to 1 c. milk. Let sit until it thickens slightly. Proceed with the recipe.

Measurement Equivalents
2 c. corn meal=10 oz
2 c. bread crumbs=8 oz
1 lb chopped nuts=2 c. packed
1 square unsweetened chocolate=1 oz
2 c. grated cheese=1 lb
8 egg whites=1 c.
16 egg yolks=1 c.
1 c. raw macaroni=2 c. cooked
1 c. raw rice=3-4 c. cooked

Alcohol Substitutions

White wine
* White grape juice
* White vinegar
* Apple juice or cider
* Lemon juice
* Pineapple juice
* Rice vinegar

Red wine
* Red or purple fruit juice
* Tea
* Vinegar
* Wine vinegar

Beer
* Ginger ale
* Apple cider or juice

Rum
*Orange juice and brown sugar

Kirsch
* Grape juice
* White vinegar
* Cherry or almond flavoring

For unto us a child is born, unto us a son is given:.
And His name shall be called Wonderful, Counselor,
the mighty God, the Everlasting Father, The Prince
of Peace.
Isaiah 9:6

Grandma Bea's Gingerbread Waffles
Yield 7-8 waffles

1/3 c. butter

2 c. flour

½ c. buttermilk

1 ½ tsp. baking soda

1 egg

1 c. molasses

½ tsp. cinnamon

2 tsp. ginger

1 tsp. salt

1. Heat the waffle iron.
2. Put butter and molasses in a pan and heat until it boils. Remove from heat and stir in milk, baking soda, and well beaten egg.
3. Sift dry ingredients and add to milk mixture.
   Continued on the next page
4. Bake in a hot waffle iron for 1 minute. Turn off the power and leave in iron for 2-3 minutes.
5. Serve with crushed fruit (Grandma would choose pineapple to go with her gingerbread.) or whipped cream.

**For unto you is born this day in the city of David
A Savior, which is Christ the Lord.
Luke 2:11**

Kaiserschmarren
Austria
Yield 4 servings

2 c. flour	¼ c. sugar
1 c. milk	½ c. butter
Pinch of salt	½ c. raisins
4 large eggs, separated	2 Tb powdered sugar
¼ c. butter, melted	stewed plums or other fruit

1. Preheat oven to 375 F.
2. Mix flour and milk to a thick paste. Add salt. Stir in 4 egg yolks and butter. Beat egg whites with sugar until stiff and fold into batter.
3. Melt ¼ c. butter in a 12" round cast iron pan or skillet. Pour the batter into the skillet. Scatter raisins over the top.
4. Bake at 375 F. for 20 minutes. Use 2 forks to tear the pancake into pieces. Dust with powdered sugar and serve with fruit.

**What can I give Him
Poor as I am?
If I were a shepard
I would bring a lamb,
If I were a Wise Man
I would do my part--
Yet what can I give Him?
Give Him my heart. Christina Rosetti**

Warm Cranberry Punch
yield 30 1/2 c. servings

1 gallon cranberry juice

15 c. water

3-4 c. sugar

½ c. lemon juice

4 whole cinnamon sticks

2 Tb whole cloves

1 nutmeg cut in ½ optional

2 c. orange juice

1. Simmer all ingredients in a large pot until it just begins to boil.
2. Remove spices.
3. Serve warm.

Raspberry Cranberry Punch
Yields 50 5 oz servings

2 ½ qt. vanilla ice cream

1 ½ gallon raspberry sherbet

1 ½ qt. cranberry juice

1 ½ qt. club soda
(or lemon lime pop)

1. Soften ice cream and sherbet.
2. Add juice and mix until well blended.
3. Add club soda (or lemon lime pop)until you get desired consistency.

A Baby's Cry
A Baby's hands in Bethlehem
Were small and softly curled.
But held within their dimpled grasp,
The Hope of all the world. (unknown)

Christmas Punch
Yield40-60 servings

3 small pk raspberry gelatin
10 c boiling water
4 c sugar
5-5 1/2 c warm water

1 (16oz) jar lemon juice
2 (46 oz) cans pineapple juice
2-3 liters ginger ale

1. Dissolve gelatin in boiling water.
2. Dissolve sugar in warm water
3. Mix all ingredients together. (not ginger ale)
4. Freeze in ice cream buckets.
5. Thaw to slush (2 ½ - 3 hours) ahead of time
6. Pour into punch bowl and add ginger ale

Over the river and through the woods,
To Grandmother's house we go,
The horse knows the way to carry the sleigh,
Through white and drifting snow.

Hot Cocoa Mix
Yield 67 servings

11 c. powdered milk

¾ c. powdered creamer

1 c. powdered sugar

16 oz instant chocolate drink
mix

1. Mix all ingredients together until well blended.
2. Store in an airtight container.
3. To make hot cocoa--mix ¼ c. mix per 1 c. hot water.

To spruce up your hot cocoa:
 Stir with a peppermint stick.
 Stir with a cinnamon stick.
 Top with a dollop of whipped cream and sprinkle
   with cinnamon.
 Pile high with marshmallows.
Get out your camera to take a photo of your very
 happy children or friends.

"Christmas banquets are probably the most fatiguing thing in the world, except for ditch digging.
Mark Twain

Spinach Dip
Yields 8 c dip

2 c. mayonnaise
16 oz sour cream
1 package frozen spinach
2 packages Knorr Vegetable
   Soup mix

8 green onions
2 small cans water chestnuts
2 loaves round rye bread

1. Drain spinach well. Mix together all ingredients--except for bread.
2. Cut the top off of the loaf of bread and cut out a round circle in the bread. Cut into cubes and allow to dry until stiff.
3. To serve--scoop the dip into the hollowed out bread, and serve with the dried bread cubes and sliced crisp vegetables.

"No man is a failure who has friends."
Clarence the angel -It's a Wonderful Life.

Peanut Butter Dip
Yields 3 1/2 c.

1 c. peanut butter   2 c. vanilla ice cream
½ c finely chopped peanuts

1. Stir peanut butter and ice cream together until ice cream melts and is blended in.
2. Pour mixture into a serving bowl.
3. Arrange sliced fruit around dip.
4. Dip fruit in the dip and then into chopped nuts.

"Miss Piggy hangs two hundred sprigs of mistletoe-- and I try to avoid them." Kermit the Frog

Cranberry Dip
Yields 1 1/2 c.

1 can cranberry sauce
2 tsp. lemon juice
¼ tsp. cinnamon

½ tsp mustard
2 Tb sugar

1. Mix well and pour into a serving dish.
2. Serve with pineapple, apples, peaches, or fried cheeses.

Fried Cheese
Yield 24 pieces

¼ c. flour
2 large eggs
1 Tb water

½ tsp seasoned salt
1 c fine bread crumbs
24 bite size cheese pieces,
(Gouda, mozzarella, cheddar)

1. Preheat the deep fryer.
2. Place flour in a shallow dish.
3. Combine eggs, water, and salt in a small bowl. Beat with a fork until well blended.
4. Place bread crumbs in a small bowl.
5. Coat cheese with flour, dip into egg mix, and then coat with bread crumbs. Repeat for a thick coating.
6. Deep fry a few pieces at a time in 375 F oil. Brown both sides. Remove with a slotted spoon and drain on paper towels. Watch closely they brown in seconds.
7. Serve with cranberry dip.

Good will toward men is the spice in the Christmas season.

Las Posadas Snack Mix
Yield 6 c.

1 can (7 ½ oz) corn chips   ¼ c. grated Parmesan
1 can (12 oz) mixed nuts   2 tsp. taco seasoning
¼ c. butter, melted

1. Preheat oven to 325 F.
2. In a large bowl, combine chips and nuts.
3. In a small bowl, combine butter, cheese, and seasoning. Pour over the chip mixture.
4. Spread evenly in a baking sheet. Bake at 325 F for 12 minutes. Cool completely, and store in an airtight container.

Las Posadas is a Mexican tradition reenacting Joseph's search for lodging.
You could have your very own Las Posadas at home.
Hide pieces of your Nativity scene around your house.
Have your children decorate a long strip of paper towels for their serapes. Use markers to make it quick and easy.
Drape the serapes over your child's shoulder and tape it together under one arm.

Lead your children around your home on a treasure hunt for the pieces of your Nativity scene.
When they collect them all, assemble your scene and eat Las Posadas snack mix.
If you're really adventurous, you could hang a pinata in your basement filled with peppermints and little Christmas trinkets.
You may like to read **The Legend of the Poinsettia** by Tomie dePaola

"The only real blind person at Christmastime is he who has not Christmas in his heart. "
Helen Keller 1906

Donkey Chow
Yield 8 c.

6 oz chocolate chips

6 c. square cereal

¼ c. peanut butter

1 c. powdered sugar

1. Melt chocolate in the microwave until lumps are gone. Add peanut butter. Stir until well blended.
2. Pour over the cereal until well coated.
3. Place the powdered sugar in a paper bag and add coated cereal. Toss well. Store in airtight container in the refrigerator.

Christmas is here, Merry old Christmas.
Gift-bearing, heart-touching,
Joy-bringing Christmas.
Day of grand memories, King of the year.
Washington Irving.

Sugared Nuts
Yield 4 1/2 c.

3 c. walnut halves

1 ½ c. pecan halves

2 c. sugar

1 c. water

¼ tsp. cinnamon

1. Preheat oven to 325 F
2. Mix all ingredients in a heavy skillet. Cook until the water disappears and the nuts have a sugary appearance.
3. Remove nuts from heat and pour onto a baking sheet. Separate nuts quickly with 2 forks.
4. Cool completely and store in an airtight container.

Creative Christmas Card display ideas

.Punch holes in each card. Use a ribbon to tie them to a grapevine wreath. Hang wreath where you will pass by often so you can smile.

.Suspend twine or cord across your mantel (or whatever mantel substitute you use.) Clip cards to the twine with clothespins painted to match your Christmas colors.

*Wrap banisters with Christmas greens. (Artificial is perfectly acceptable.) Hang cards from greens with gold ribbons.

*Put cards in a basket on your table. Each evening, read the cards that arrived that day. Pray for the friend that sent it to you.

Creamy Dip
Yield 2 c.

1 c. cottage cheese   1 envelope ranch dressing

1 c. sour cream

1. Mix all together and refrigerate.
2. Serve with crackers.

To use up leftover non-alcoholic egg nog, replace milk with egg nog. It's great in pancakes, French toast, quick breads, cookies, and muffins.

Some people don't like the commercial egg nog--or egg milk as my son calls it--but we think it's yummy.

We serve it in a crystal goblet with freshly grated nutmeg on the top.

Light a candle, turn on the Christmas carols, and enjoy.

Meat
&
Side Dishes

Turkey Tips

*Frozen whole turkeys may be stored in the original wrapper for up to 12 months at 0 F or lower.

How much to buy?

*Whole turkey--from 4 ½ lbs to 24 lbs. allow 1 to 1 ½ lbs. per person.
*Breast of turkey--from 3-9 lbs--allow ¾ lb per person.
*Boneless breast of turkey--from 2 ¾ to 3 ½ lbs--allow ½ lb per person.

How long will it take?

Weight (lbs)	Stuffed (hours)	Unstuffed (hours)
6-8	3-3 ½	2 ½-3 ½
8-12	3 ½ -4 ½	3-4
12-16	4-5	3 ½-4 ½
16-20	4 ½-5 ½	4-5
20-24	5-6 ½	4 ½-5 ½

Is it done yet?

*Insert meat thermometer into the meatiest part of the thigh without touching the bone. It should read 180-185 F.
*Stuffing temperature should read 160-165 F
*Turkey juices should run clear.
*Drumsticks should move up and down easily. (Just don't start waving at the children with them. They will think you've gone mad.)

Milanesa--Argentina
Yield 4 servings

3 garlic cloves, minced
½ tsp salt
1 tsp oregano
¾ lb bread crumbs

3 eggs
4 Steaks, ¾" thick
Oil for frying

1. Mix garlic, salt, and oregano in a medium bowl.
2. Place the bread crumbs on a large plate.
3. Crack the eggs into the spices. Mix well.
4. Start heating the oil in a skillet.
5. Dip the steaks into the egg mixture and then into the bread crumbs on both sides.
6. Fry in skillet 4-5 minutes on each side. Or until desired doneness is reached.

**Milanesa (Breaded Steak) is commonly served with either french fried or mashed potatoes, and a salad.

The average American in his life will eat 14 cattle!

An old tin grater makes a beautiful decoration. Light a tea light or votive candle and set the tin grater over the top of the candle. The holes in the grater allow the light to glimmer in charming patterns.

Mediterranean Meatballs
Yield 18 meatballs

Meatballs:

1 ¼ lb ground turkey
¼ c chopped onion
1 ½ tsp oregano
1 tsp. lemon juice

½ tsp each dried mint, parsley,
    & lemon pepper
1 clove garlic, minced

Sauce:

½ c Sour Cream
½ medium cucumber,
   chopped finely

1 ½ tsp lemon juice
1/8 tsp pepper

1. Combine meatball ingredients; mix well. Shape into 18 balls.
   Cook meatballs in a non-stick skillet 8-10 minutes, or until
   browned through the center. Stir occasionally.
2. Combine sauce ingredients.
3. Serve over lettuce and tomatoes, or rice.

Easy Christmas Eve Lasagna
Yield 8 servings

1 16 oz box lasagna, cook as directed on package
1 1/2 lb ground beef browned with 1 medium chopped onion
Add 1 jar –32 oz –spaghetti sauce to beef
Salt and pepper to taste
Mozzarella cheese 1 ½ lbs sliced or grated

1. In a large cake pan,(9×13) place alternate layers of lasagna , sauce and
beef mix, mozzarella cheese.
2.Bake 350 f for 30 minutes

Mom's Green Bean Casserole
Yields 6 servings

1 pkg. 16 oz French cut green beans

1 can French fried onion rings

1 can (10 oz) cream of mushroom soup

1. Preheat oven to 325 F.
2. Mix green beans with soup and ½ can of the onions.
3. Bake at 325 F for 30 minutes.
4. Top with the remaining onions and bake for 15 more minutes.

Christmas is coming
The goose is getting fat,
Please put a penny
In the Old man's hat.
If you haven't got a penny
A ha'penny will do,
If you haven't got a ha'penny
God bless you!

Bruna Bonor--Swedish Brown Beans
Yields 4 servings

2 c. red kidney beans

5 c. water

Salt to taste

¼ c. dark corn syrup

¼ c. vinegar, or to taste

1. Rinse dry beans and place in a pot with the water. Salt to taste. Simmer until tender 1-2 hours. Add more water as needed.
2. When beans are cooked, add the syrup and vinegar. Adjust seasonings if desired.
3. Serve steaming hot.

**Can be prepared the day before.

**My mom boils a pot of water as the beans are cooking so that when she adds more water to the beans it's boiling hot and does not stop the cooking process.

"The Christmas tree was at least 15 feet tall. The Captain took care of the top, while Baroness Matilda and I busied ourselves with the lower branches. There were cookies, Lebkuchen, and Spanischer Wind. Hard candies and chocolates had been wrapped in frilled tissue paper, figures and symbols made of marzipan, gilded nuts, and small apples and tangerines--all were hung on red threads all over the tree. Then came a hundred and twenty wax candles, loads of tinsels, and tinsel chains and a large silver star which the Captain fastened to the very top. Then we all stepped back and admired the most beautiful Christmas tree we had ever seen.   Maria von Trapp

Golden Fan Potatoes~Quebec
Yield: 12 servings

12 medium potatoes, peeled   ¼ c. butter
Paprika

1. Cut down through the top of each potato, making thin slices but keep the potato together by not slicing through the bottom. (Leave ¼" uncut). Place potatoes in a bowl of cold water and cover with ice cubes. Let stand 1 hour.
2. Drain potatoes and dry. Roll in paprika until well coated.
3. Melt butter in a large frying pan and cook potatoes uncovered over low heat. Turn them often until tender and golden brown 35-40 minutes. The cut side of the potato will open like a fan.
4. Serve on a large platter with a paper fan by each one with good wishes personally written to each guest.

While Thanksgiving has its foundation on Plymouth Rock,
Christmas rests upon the Rock of Ages.
Charles Dudley Warner

Cheese Potatoes
Yield 4-6 servings

3 large potatoes, sliced
Pepper to taste
Salt to taste
1 large onion, sliced

5 bacon slices, cooked
½ c. butter, melted
½ lb sharp cheddar, cubed

1. Preheat oven to 350 F.
2. Slice potato into a large piece of foil. Sprinkle with pepper and salt. Crumble bacon over potatoes. Add onion and cheese. Dot with butter.
3. Wrap foil loosely around the potatoes and seal with a double fold.
4. Bake at 350 F for 1 hour.

If we could condense all the truths of Christmas into only three words, these would be the words: "God with us." We tend to focus our attention at Christmas on the infancy of Christ. The greater truth of the holiday is His deity. More astonishing than a baby in the manger is the truth that this promised baby is the omnipotent Creator of the heavens and the earth!

John F. MacArthur, Jr.

Grandma's Sweet potato casserole
Yield 6-8 servings

3 c. sweet potatoes
 (cooked and mashed)
2 eggs

1 tsp vanilla
 Cinnamon & Nutmeg to taste
1c. sugar

Topping:

1 c. brown sugar
½ stick butter

1 c. chopped pecans
3 Tb. Flour

1. Combine sweet potatoes and all casserole ingredients.
   place in oven proof baking dish.
2. Mix sugar, pecans, and flour. I like to add cinnamon and nutmeg
   here too. Cover sweet potato mixture with topping and dot with
   butter.

3. Bake at 450 F 30-45 minutes.
**You can probably use less sugar in here and it will still be yummy.

When my dad was growing up, they never ate sweet
potatoes as a vegetable. Only as dessert.
He still turns up his nose if sweet potatoes are
served with the meal.
When we were children, I'd watch him refuse to eat
them for dinner, but eat a baked sweet potato with
cinnamon on top for dessert.

Rachel's Stuffing
Yield 10 servings

1 large can of chicken broth   1 c. shredded carrots
1/2 cup chopped celery   ½ c. finely chopped onions
Poultry seasoning to taste   1 lb butter NO MARGARINE
1-2 bags of stuffing cubes

1. Pour broth in a large pan. Add carrots, celery, onions, butter, and poultry seasoning Bring to a boil and let boil until all ingredients are very soft.
2. Pour ¾ a bag of stuffing cubes into a large bowl. Pour broth mixture over the cubes.....add more stuffing cubes a small amount at a time until stuffing reaches desired consistency.
3. Serve with your turkey dinner.

**I made this for Thanksgiving this year. Wow! It was so yummy. Rachel learned this recipe while working in a restaurant.

The hinge of history is on the door of a Bethlehem stable.

Ralph W Sockman

Cookies, Desserts, & Candies

Jumballs
England
Yield 24

1 c. flour
¾ c. powdered sugar
¼ almonds, ground

½ tsp. vanilla, or almond
1 egg white
2-4 tsp. cream

1. Preheat oven to 450 F.
2. Sift flour and powdered sugar, and add ground almonds.
   Mix as you would pie crust. Add flavoring, and unbeaten
   egg white. Add just enough cream to make a stiff paste.
3. Roll dough thin on a floured board. Cut in fancy shapes and
   bake at 450 F for 10 minutes or until lightly browned.
   Watch carefully, they burn quickly.
4. When baked, dust with powdered sugar. These keep well in a tin.

This recipe was adapted from a book printed in 1797
"The Art of Cookery Made Plain and Easy" by Hannah Glasse.

In Russia, the Babushka misdirected the wise Men and refused to shelter the Holy Family when they fled to Egypt. Now she travels through Russia knocking at each door, entering and holding a candle close to each child's face as he sleeps. After slipping a toy under the pillow, she hurries away searching for the Babe of Bethlehem, whom she has never found.

Moravian Cookies
Yield 100

Mix the dough a couple of weeks before you desire to bake cookies.

¼ c. butter, melted

½ c. molasses, heated

¼ c. brown sugar

1/3 tsp. ginger

1/3 tsp. cloves

1/3 tsp. cinnamon

1/8 tsp. nutmeg

1/8 tsp. allspice

dash of salt

1/3 tsp baking soda

2 c. flour

1. Combine butter, and molasses, add sugar, spices, salt, and baking soda. Add flour gradually, mixing well.
2. Let stand for 10 days in a cold place.
3. Preheat oven to 375 F.
4. Roll dough paper thin and cut in fancy shapes. Bake at 375 F for 6 minutes.

"Christmas morning broke on a beautiful white world. It had been a very mild December and people had looked forward to a green Christmas; but just enough snow fell softly in the night to transfigure Avonlea. Anne peeped out from her frosted gable window with delighted eyes. She ran downstairs singing until her voice re-echoed through Green Gables.

'Merry Christmas, Marilla! Merry Christmas, Matthew! Isn't it a lovely Christmas? I'm so glad it's white. Another kind of Christmas doesn't' seem real,."

The Best Sugar Cookies Ever!
Yield 2 dozen

1 ½ c. powdered sugar
1 c. butter
1 egg
1 tsp. vanilla

2 ½ c. flour
1 tsp. baking soda
1 tsp. cream of tarter
   optional but hold dough
   together better

1. Preheat oven to 375 F.
2. Cream powdered sugar, butter, egg, and vanilla.
3. Add flour, baking soda, and cream of tarter.
4. Roll dough out and cut with cookie cutters.

"Every time a bell rings, an angel gets his wings."
Zuzu It's a Wonderful Life

Joyce's Brown Sugar Cookies
Yield 2-4 dozen

½ c. butter
1 c. brown sugar
1 egg
1 tsp. vanilla

1 tsp. orange rind, grated
1 ¾ c. flour
¼. tsp salt
1 tsp. baking powder

1. Preheat oven to 375 F.
2. Beat together butter, sugar, eggs, vanilla, and orange rind.
3. Combine flour, salt, and baking powder. Add to sugar mixture.
   Mix well.
4. Chill dough for several hours or overnight.
5. Roll out and cut in shapes. Place on ungreased cookie sheets.
6. Bake at 375 F 6-8 minutes.
7. Cool and decorate as you would sugar cookies, or glaze.

Grandma's Goodies
Yield 30 squares

½ c. butter, softened
12 oz. chunky peanut butter
2 c. powdered sugar

2 c. crisp rice cereal
12 oz. chocolate chips

1. Mix butter, peanut butter, powdered sugar, and cereal.
2. Press mixture down into an ungreased 8"x8" pan.
3. Melt chocolate chips and pour over the top of goodies. Let cool and cut into small squares.

The holly and the ivy,
When they are both full grown,
Of all the trees that are in the wood,
The holly bears the crown.

Mom's Spicy Gingerbread Boys
Yield 24 boys (5" cutter)

2 c. flour
½. tsp. salt
½ tsp. baking soda
1 tsp. baking powder
1 tsp. ginger
1 tsp. cloves

1 ½ tsp. cinnamon
½ tsp. nutmeg
1 c. shortening
½ c. sugar
½ c. molasses
1 egg yolk

1. Mix dough early in the day. Sift flour with salt, baking soda, baking powder, ginger, cloves, cinnamon, and nutmeg.
2. In a large bowl, cream shortening with sugar and molasses until light and fluffy. Beat in egg yolk, and flour mixture. Refrigerate all day.

Gingerbread boys continued

3. Roll out dough on a floured surface. Cut out gingerbread boys. Place on an ungreased cookie sheet.
4. Bake at 350 F for 8-10 minutes.

When we were children, baking gingerbread boys was the highlight of our Christmas season. Spicy smells wafted through the kitchen as we helped mom roll and cut out our special cookies. When they had cooled, the fun began.

Mom purchased all sorts of icing in tubes for outlining the boys. Cinnamon red hots, and white frosting were also part of the fun.

We took our gingerbread boy decorating very seriously spending hours making them just right. Of course we'd eat two or three while we laughed and expressed our creativity. Then we'd tuck them away in their tin saving some for another day.

A Merry Christmas TO YOU.

Cowboy Cookies
Yield 8 dozen
Our family's Christmas Must Have

1 c. shortening	2 c. flour
1 c. white sugar	1 tsp. baking powder
1 c. brown sugar	1 tsp. salt
½ c. peanut butter	½ tsp. baking soda
2 eggs	2 c. oatmeal
1 tsp. vanilla	12 oz. chocolate chips

1. Preheat oven to 350 F.
2. Cream together shortening, sugars and peanut butter. Add eggs and vanilla.
3. Combine the dry ingredients and add to the creamed mixture.
3. Add the oatmeal and chocolate chips.
4. Bake at 350 F on ungreased baking sheets for 8-12 minutes. You can freeze them ahead of time. They store well…if any are leftover!

"Christmas Day should be fragrant with the love that we bear one another. It is good to be children sometimes, and never better than at Christmas, when it's Mighty Founder was a Child himself.
Charles Dickens

Dorothy's Toffee Squares
Yield 24 squares

½ c. butter

½ c. shortening

1 c. brown sugar

1 egg

1 tsp. vanilla

½ tsp. salt

2 c. flour

12 oz. chocolate chips

1. Preheat oven to 325 F.
2. Cream together butter, shortening, and sugar. Add egg and vanilla, mix 'til creamy.
3. Add salt and flour. Stir together.
4. Pat dough into a 8"x 8" pan.
5. Bake at 325 F for 15-20 minutes.
6. Spread melted chocolate chips over warm baked bars.

It is Christmas in the Mansion
Yule-log fires and silken frocks.
It is Christmas in the Cottage,
Mother is filling socks.

For a fun Christmas table setting, use a brightly colored knit scarf as a table runner. Put silverware in coordinating knit mittens tied with a ribbon.

Grandma's Sweet Potato Pie
Yield 1 pie

3 large sweet potatoes   ½ c. brown sugar
½ tsp. nutmeg   ½ c. coconut
½ c. butter   1 9" pie shell, unbaked
2 eggs   coconut to sprinkle on top

1. Preheat oven to 350 F
2. Cook potatoes, peel and mash. Add all ingredients but pie shell.
   Mix well and pour into pie shell. Sprinkle with coconut.
3. Bake at 350 F. for 1 hour or until golden brown.
** Grandma's secret *"Don't measure anything. Just make everything to taste."*

Bohemian Winter Song
Drop down, drop down, white snowflakes!
We shall hide ourselves in fur coats
And when the blizzard comes
We shall put on fur caps,
We shall harness our golden sleighs,
We shall drive down from our hillside.
And if we fall into a snowdrift
We hope that the wind will not cover us.
So that we can drive back quickly
For the fairy tales
Which Grandfather will tell us.

Pecan Pie
Another Christmas Must Have
Yield 1 pie

3 eggs, slightly beaten

1 c. corn syrup

1 c. sugar

2 Tb. butter, melted

1 tsp. vanilla

1 ½ c. pecans

1 9" pie shell, unbaked

1. Preheat oven to 350 F.
2. Stir eggs, corn syrup, sugar, butter, and vanilla together until well blended. Stir in pecans.
3. Pour into unbaked pie shell. Bake at 350 F for 50-55 minutes. Check for doneness by sticking a knife in the pie. If it comes out clean, it's done. If not, let it bake 10 more minutes and check again.

Pumpkin Pie
Yield 1 pie

2 eggs

1 can (16 oz.) pumpkin

¾ c. sugar

½ tsp. salt

1 9" pie shell, unbaked

1 tsp. cinnamon

½ tsp. ginger

¼ tsp. cloves

1 can (12 oz) evaporated milk.

1. Preheat oven to 425 F.
2. Beat eggs. Stir in remaining ingredients.
3. Pour into pie shell. Bake for 15 minutes at 425 F.
4. Reduce heat to 350 F. Bake 40-45 minutes

Creamy Pumpkin Pie
Yield 1 pie

1 c. canned pumpkin

½ c. cold milk

1 pkg. (6 servings) instant
  vanilla pudding

1 tsp. pumpkin pie spice

3 ½ c. whipped topping

1 9" graham cracker crust

1. Combine pumpkin, milk, pudding mix and spice in a small bowl.
   Blend with a whisk for 1 minute.
2. Fold in 2 ½ c. whipped topping. Spoon into pie crust.
   Freeze until firm, about 4 hours.
3. Top with remaining whipped topping before serving.

Yellow stars like lamps, blue stars like icicles, twinkled up above and far away across the valley. A running star showed a cart or gig traveling along the coach road, where the cathedral stood, and the big market and fine shops.

Susan pressed her nose to the cold window-pane until it became a flat white button, and her breath froze into feathery crystals. "This is Christmas Day, it's Christmas Day, it won't come again for a whole year. "It's Christmas," she murmured.

Allison Utley <u>A Country Child</u>

Epiphany Cake
(or Kings & Queen Cake
Or Twelfth Night Cake)

Choose any favorite cake recipe.
Wrap the following items in foil and insert into the batter before baking.

Button--faithfulness   Ring--faithfulness
Dime--wealth   Thimble--patience
Bean--king   Pea--queen
Heart--devotion   Clove--fool, jester

The finder of each item is supposed to reflect the qualities or capabilities the token is whimsically said to represent.

Parties celebrating Twelfth Night were held January 5th to bring the Christmas season to a close. To furnish a game, a special cake was served that day.
The man who found the bean was crowned King and could choose a Queen. Or the woman who found the pea was crowned Queen and could choose a King.

Julgrot
Sweden
Yield 8 servings

¾ c rice, uncooked　　　　　1 tsp. vanilla
½ tsp. salt　　　　　　　　　1/3 c. raisins
4 eggs　　　　　　　　　　　1 whole almond
1/3 c. sugar　　　　　　　　　cinnamon, sugar, cream
3 c. milk, heat to lukewarm

1. Preheat oven to 350F
2. In a saucepan, combine rice with 1 ½ c water and salt. Bring to a boil, stir, and reduce heat to low. Cover and simmer 20 minutes until rice has absorbed the water.
3. Whisk together eggs, sugar, warmed milk, and vanilla. Add rice and raisins. Turn into a 2 quart buttered baking dish. Bury the almond in the pudding.
4. Place the dish in a larger pan of boiling water. Bake at 350 F uncovered for 1 hour or until the pudding is set. Stir once or twice during baking and before serving.
5. Serve hot with cinnamon, sugar, and cream.

There are 2 ways to play this game:

1. Whoever gets the almond gets to pass out the Christmas gifts.

2. Bury several almonds and the first unmarried person to find and almond will be the next one to be married.

Kiesiel Zurawinowi--Cranberry Dessert
Poland
Yield 4 servings

1 lb fresh cranberries
½ c. sugar

¼ c. potato flour or
  cornstarch

1. Boil cranberries briskly in 1 3/4c. Water until skins burst.
2. Rub cooked berries through a sieve. Return puree to the pot and add sugar. Mix flour with a little water and stir into the puree.
3. Bring to a boil, reduce heat and cook gently until it thickens.
4. Serve chilled with whip cream.

At Christmas time in Poland, the table is covered with a white cloth for good luck and set with extra places for absent family members. A special place is set for the Christ Child.

1.2 billion candy canes are made for the Christmas season. That is enough to circle the globe three times.

Leah's Three Layer Brownies
Yield 12

Brownies:

2 squares unsweetened chocolate
1/3 c. butter
1 c. sugar
2 eggs

1 tsp vanilla
2/3 c. flour
½ tsp salt

Filling:

¼ c. butter
2 c. powdered sugar

2 Tb milk
½ tsp. vanilla

Topping:

1 square unsweetened chocolate   1 Tb butter

1. Melt unsweetened chocolate and butter in the microwave for 3 minutes. Add sugar, eggs, and vanilla. Mix well. Add flour and salt. Pour into a greased 9" microwavable pan.
2. Microwave for 2 minutes, rotate and microwave for 2 minutes. Wile brownies are cooling, make the filling.
3. Microwave butter for 5 minutes, or until browned (cover so that it will not splatter.) Add powdered sugar, milk, and vanilla. Pour on the bottom layer.
4. Melt the chocolate and butter for the topping and pour over the filling. Refrigerate for 2-3 hours to allow the brownies to set.

"Each man's life touches so many other lives."
Clarence the Angel
It's a Wonderful Life

Perfect Pound Cake
Yield 1 cake

8 oz cream cheese
4 sticks real butter
3 c sugar

6 eggs
3 c all purpose flour
1 Tb vanilla

1. Combine cream cheese and butter til fluffy, then add sugar and blend well.
2. Add each egg separately and blend thoroughly (this is key!) add vanilla.
3. Add flour and salt a little at a time until blended thoroughly .
4. Pour into a bundt pan or 2 loaf pans --greased very well but do not use butter
5. Bake for 1 hour and 30 minutes at 350 f

"A merry Christmas, Uncle!" "Bah! Humbug!" said Scrooge.
"Christmas a humbug, Uncle! You don't mean that, I am sure?"
"I do. Merry Christmas! What reason do you have to be merry? You're poor enough."
"I have always thought of Christmas time, when it has come round as a good time; a kind, forgiving, charitable, pleasant time; the only time I know of, when men and women seem to open their shut-up hearts freely, and to think of people below them. Therefore, Uncle, though it has never put a scrap of gold or silver in my pocket, I believe that is has done me good, and will do me good; and I say, God bless it!"

A Merry Christmas
TO YOU.

Vintage Molasses Cake
Yield 1 9"x13" cake

½ c. shortening

½ c. sugar

3 eggs, beaten

¾ tsp. baking soda

2/3 c. molasses

2 ¼ c. flour

1 tsp. cinnamon

¼ tsp. cloves

¼ tsp. mace

1 tsp. salt

½ c. milk

½ c. raisins

1. Preheat oven to 350 F.
2. Cream shortening and sugar; add beaten eggs and mix well.
3. Mix the baking soda with the molasses, and add to the shortening mixture.
4. Sift the flour, cinnamon, cloves, mace, and salt.
5. Add the flour mixture alternately with the milk to the shortening mixture. Beat thoroughly.
6. Stir the raisins into the mixture.
7. Pour into a greased 9"x 13" pan.
8. Bake at 350 F for 40-50 minutes.

This is adapted from a 1926 cookbook. My Grandma (born in 1920), adores this cake. She likes to top it with crushed pineapple.

Jo's Apple Slices
Yield 24 slices

2 ½ c. sifted flour

1 Tb. Sugar

1 tsp. salt

1 c. lard

1 egg, separated

Milk

2/3 c. crushed cornflakes

5 c. sliced apples

1 ½ c. sugar

1 tsp. cinnamon

1. Preheat oven to 400 F
2. Sift flour, salt, and sugar. Cut into lard as you would for pie crust.
3. Put egg yolk in a cup and add milk to make ¾ c. Add to lard mixture. Mix just enough until dough shapes into a ball.
4. Divide dough into 2 rolls, each half to make a 15" x 11" rectangle.
5. Transer to cookie sheet, spread on corn flakes. Add apples and sprinkle with sugar & cinnamon.
6. Top with the 2nd crust.
7. Bake at 400 F for 40 minutes.
8. While hot, drizzle with powdered sugar glaze. (Just powdered sugar with a couple tablespoons of milk to make a thin glaze.

Candy Temperatures Chart

Temperature	Stage	When dropped into Very cold water:
234-240 F	soft ball	Forms a soft ball which flattens on removal from water.
244-248 F	firm ball	Forms a firm ball which does not flatten on removal from water.
250-266 F	hard ball	Forms a firm ball which is hard enough to hold its shape, yet is pliable.
270-290 F	soft crack	Separates into threads which are hard but not brittle.
300-310 F	hard crack	Separates into threads wich are hard and brittle.

Turtles
Yield 50 candies

1 can sweetened condensed milk   Pecans

1 c. white corn syrup   1 bag chocolate stars

1. Cook milk and corn syrup together over low heat until caramel colored and thick--25 minutes.
2. Pour 1 Tbsp. caramel mixture over a cluster of 2 pecans on a greased cookie sheet.
3. Put one chocolate star on the top of each cluster. After it has melted, spread it out with the back of a spoon.
4. Let cool, and then store in an airtight container.

Bring forth the fir tree,
The box and they bay,
Deck out our cottage
For glad Christmas day.
Old English

Super Easy Fudge
Yield 6 lbs.

1 lb cream cheese	1 c. cocoa
1 lb butter	1 c. nuts
4 lbs powdered sugar	

1. Melt cream cheese and butter in a large stockpot.
2. Add powdered sugar and cocoa. Mix well with hands. This one is fun for the children.
3. Press into glass pans (or tins for gift giving).
4. Refrigerate for 30 minutes. (Story on the next page)

This recipe came to us after what we call "The Great Fudge experiment". My mom had tried a new fudge recipe every year. Nothing was turning out right. Some were like frosting,, others were like thick chocolate soup--we actually ate that fudge with a spoon that year. Someone shared this with my mom and it's been our fudge recipe for more than 20 years. It never messes up and it tastes so good!

May thy Christmas happy be,
And naugh but joy appear,
Is now the wish I send to thee,
And all I loves most dear.
Victorian Christmas Carol

Christmas Bark
Yield 1 lb

1 lb white almond bark   extra mint pieces
1/3 c. crushed peppermint pieces
      (red and green)

1. Melt almond bark; stir crushed candy into the bark. Pour out onto waxed paper and spread to ¼ to 1/8" thin.
2. Sprinkle additional peppermint pieces on top before almond bark sets.
3. Cool and break into pieces.

Miscellaneous

Apple Cinnamon Dough

1 cup cinnamon
1 cup apple sauce
1 -2 plastics zip bag

1. Pour cinnamon and applesauce into a zip bag.

2. Seal the zip bag and knead until the mixture turns to dough.

3. Roll some dough out about 1/4 inch thick, then use cookie cutters to create fragrant tree ornaments, package ties, and air fresheners. Make a small hole toward the top of your cut-out before the dough dries so that it can be hung with string or ribbon.
Applesauce cinnamon dough can also be molded by pushing it into candy and popcorn molds.

4. Allow your applesauce cinnamon dough creations to air-dry for 12 hours or until hard.
** I think it takes much longer to dry. I put them on a cookie cooling rack so both sides could be exposed to the air.

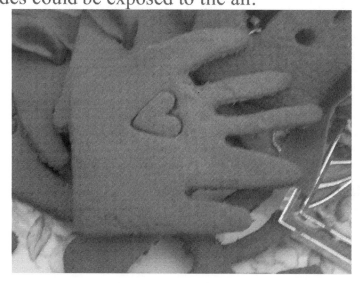

China White Decorations
Yield 10 ornaments

1 c. cornstarch   1 ¼ c. cold water

2 c. baking soda

1. In a saucepan, combine starch and baking soda. Gradually add water until mixture is smooth. Heat, stirring constantly until the mixture reaches a moist, mashed potato consistency.
2. Turn onto a plate. Cover with a damp towel. Knead dough when it is cool enough to handle.
3. Roll to ¼" thickness. Dip cutters in cornstarch before cutting.
4. Allow to dry for several days at room temperature on a rack to allow circulation. Pierce with a straw before drying if you are planning to hang the ornament.

The ornaments of a home are the friends who frequent it.

Baker's Clay Ornaments
Yield 15 ornaments

4 c. flour   1 ½ c. water

1 c. salt

1. Combine flour and salt. Gradually add water until mixture is like putty. Knead dough for 5 minutes.
2. Roll out to ¼" thickness on a floured surface. Cut with cookie cutters dipped in flour.
3. Bake on ungreased cookie sheet at 325 F for ½ hour or until light brown--or air dry on a rack for 48 hours. Pierce with a straw if you are planning to hang the ornament.'

Ornament Tips

**Use an emery board to smooth roughness after drying.
**Coat with a thin shellac.
**Paint with water colors, or acrylic paints and coat with shellac.
**Cover areas with a thin coat of white glue and then sprinkle with glitter.
**Sign and date ornaments.

The rooms were very still while the pages were softly turned and the winter sunshine crept in to touch the bright heads and serious faces with a Christmas greeting.
-- **Louisa May Alcott**

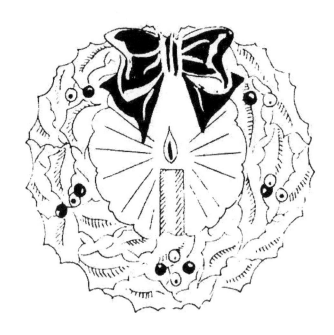

Gourmet Dog Biscuits
Yield 20

1 c. wheat flour   1 Tbsp brown sugar
1 c. white flour   6 Tbsp butter
½ c. wheat germ   1 egg
½ c. powdered milk

1. Preheat oven to 325 F.
2. Combine flours, wheat germ, milk, and brown sugar. Cut in
   Butter until it's like cornmeal.
3. Add egg and enough water to form a stiff dough.
4. Knead on a floured surface. Roll to desired thickness and cut
   Into shapes.
5. Bake at 325 F for 30-40 minutes. Serve cool.
**Since these are all natural you may want to store them in the
   refrigerator. Just trust me!

A wreath in your window and goodwill in your
Heart make a very merry Christmas!

Some of our Family Traditions

1. A child friendly Nativity scene to allow little hands to explore and share in the Christmas story.

2. Read a different Christmas book every day.

3. Baby socks advent calendar. Choose one baby sock for each day until Christmas. Fill with a couple pieces of candy, or a tiny toy. Add a slip of paper with a Christmas joke or things like,
" No chores today" or "Choose a game we can play together". Hang by clothes pins on a ribbon or garland and choose one per day.

4. Drive around and look at the lights.

5. Bake a special cookie or treat allowing the children to help.

6. Fill the home with the beautiful sounds of Christmas music.

**Add your traditions on the following page.

Our Traditions

1.

2.

3.

4.

5.

6.

7.

8.

9.

10.

**Notes

Snow Day Ideas

*Go sledding

*Drink Hot cocoa

*Cuddle on the couch under your favorite quilt and tell stories from your childhood.

* Watch Christmas movies.

* Make thank you cards for sending out after Christmas.

* Get out the play dough.

*Fill a spray bottle with water and food coloring. Send it outside with your children so they can "paint" the snow.

*Read your favorite books together.

* Make wrapping paper. Stamp or color on the inside of brown paper grocery bags.

* Choose a recipe from this book to make together.
Make sure to snack on it!

A charming Christmas garland can be made from twine and scrap fabric.
Cut or tear fabric into strips from approximately 4" to 6".
   Tie the rag strips onto the twine. Knot tightly and bunch them close together.
Continue until the garland is as long as you desire.

Winds through the olive trees
Softly did blow
'Round little Bethlehem
Long, long ago.

Sheep on the hillside lay
Whiter than snow.
Shepherds were watching them
Long, long ago.

Then from the midnight sky
Angels bent low.
Singing their songs of joy
Long, long ago.

Soft in a manger bed
Cradled so low,
Christ came to Bethlehem
Long, long ago.

Our favorite Children's Christmas Books

1. A Charlie Brown Christmas Charles Schultz

2. Red Boots for Christmas adapted by Carol Greene

3. The Truth about Santa Claus (When your child is ready to Hear) Alan Barrington

4. The Gingerbread Man retold by Jim Aylesworth

5. Merry Christmas Mom and Dad Mercer Mayer

6. Christmas in Noisy Village Astrid Lindgren

7. The Wild Christmas Reindeer Jan Brett

8. Gingerbread Baby Jan Brett

9. Trouble with Trolls Jan Brett

10. Baboushka and the Three Kings Ruth Robbins

11. Frosty the Snowman

12. The Christmas Miracle of Jonathan Toomey Susan Wojciechowski (The illustrations are gorgeous.)

13. The Best Christmas Pageant Ever Barbara Robinson

14. The Legend of the Candy Cane Lori Walburg

15. The Tale of Three Trees retold by Angela Elwell Hunt

16. The Snowman Storybook Raymond Briggs

My favorite Christmas Books

1. Christmas Joy Susan Branch

2. Shepherds Abiding Jan Karon

3. Esther's Gift Jan Karon

4. Homespun Christmas by Gooseberry Patch

Thank you for sharing some of my favorite
Christmas recipes and traditions.
Visit me online at
<u>www.adustyframe.com</u>

Love,
Lizzie

Made in the USA
Las Vegas, NV
05 December 2023